WHEN LOVE POURS, LOVE Speaks

DAILY DEVOTION

AMANDA NABORS

"Quote Queen"

HOV
PUBLISHING

HOV Publishing is a division of HOV, LLC.
Email: hopeofvision@gmail.com
www.hovpub.com

Cover Design and Layout: HOV Designs
Editor: HOV Publishing editing team

Contact the Author:
Amanda Nabors, "Quote Queen"
hisjoy@bellsouth.net

For further information regarding special discounts on bulk purchases, please contact: Amanda Nabors at hisjoy@bellsouth.net.

ISBN Paperback: 978-1-955107-52-5
ISBN eBook: 978-1-955107-51-8

Printed in the United States of America

- ENDORSEMENTS -

I am honored and blessed to endorse this woman of love, a woman of God, and my sister, Amanda Nabors.

Love is the key because the love of God is poured out into our hearts by the Holy Spirit, given to us by God. God is love. We love because He first loved us. Love is the key. You plant your flowers and watch them grow. Love is the key. You've got to have the key to open up the door. God is love. Love is God.
Love is the key.

Evangelist Michael Hondreau Rudolph
Co-founder of Commission of Faith,
Evangelistic Outreach Ministry

Love is the universal language that speaks to the secret place of the human soul if allowed. In a world filled with extreme hatred, chaos, and confusion, Minister Amanda has timelessly and strategically deployed a book that weaves love, which is the essence of who God is. Throughout the pages, vibrant threads are woven predicated upon her relationship with God, her life experiences, and her memories as she travels along her life's journey.

Minister Amanda's book, When Love Pours, Love Speaks, will bless and edify the readers and ignite the beginning of a healing balm in our homes, communities, and land.

Mrs. Evelyn Jones

Publisher Endorsement

It is with great admiration that I endorse Amanda Nabors as the undisputed *Quote Queen*. In her soul-stirring book *When Love Pours, Love Speaks*, Amanda delivers a treasury of heartfelt wisdom, each quote flowing like poetry and truth. Her words don't just speak, they pour into the soul, leaving a lasting imprint of love, healing, and empowerment. This is more than a book; it's a movement, and Amanda Nabors is its voice.

Germaine Miller-Summers
CEO, HOV Publishing a division of HOV, LLC.

- DEDICATION -

I want to dedicate this book to my dear Pastors, Joe and Shawnneice Brock, and to all who have spoken words of love, encouragement, truth, strength, and wisdom into my life. To my daughter Kristen, who is a gift of love and exemplifies love's strength, giving, hope, and endurance. To Abba Father, who loves me with an everlasting love and kisses me daily with the sweetness of His love, kindness, and compassion.

The name Amanda means "Worthy of Love, Beloved." The Father wanted me to know that I am worthy of love, and He inscribed it upon my entire being. His love conveys my worth, not predicated on my performance, capabilities, or talents.

What a joy to experience and know that I am accepted in the beloved for ALL eternity! The Father's love never looks for a reason to love or love on us. Everything about His love is unconditionally given; by His love, we are fearfully and wondrously made!

Every facet of our being reflects His love and His passionate desire for us. Through pain, fear, trials, mistakes, heartaches, disappointments, and setbacks, His love can speak to every situation so that we can embrace healing, restoration, peace, wholeness, life, and life more abundantly.

Every day, His amazing love celebrates us, and the radiance of love's beauty is limitless! Oh, how He loves you and me!

As you reflect upon these words, may you truly embrace love and know your heart is the cup designed for love to be poured in and poured out, loving out Loud!

- SCRIPTURES -

For God so loved the world, that He gave His only begotten Son, that whosoever believeth in Him should not perish, but have everlasting life (John 3:16).

Be kindly affectioned one to another with brotherly love; in honour preferring one another (Romans 12:10).

There is no fear in love; but perfect love casteth out fear: because fear hath torment. He that feareth is not made perfect in love (1 John 4:18).

For God hath not given us the spirit of fear; but of power, and of love, and of a sound mind (2 Timothy 1:7).

- FOREWORD -

From the first day we met, I realized there was something extraordinarily unique about Minister Amanda Nabors. It was not merely her kind smile and engaging eyes; it was the light that exuded from her very presence—the light of the love of God. It was clear to me that this woman of God possessed a special grace—a God-given grace. Amanda has the gift of love. Out of that gift, as an ordained minister, Amanda preaches and teaches the gospel and is also a prayer counselor extraordinaire.

This world is hungry, and many are searching to fill that void. Seekers have no idea that their hunger is for the "Living Bread" (Jn.6:51). In this prolific love text, When Love Pours, Love Speaks, Amanda shows forth the love of God in a simplistic yet eloquent manner. As the Apostle Paul describes it, the reader will discover that the "greatest gift," love (1 Cor. 13:13), resonates on every page.

It is commendable to have a prayer meeting, but it is even more essential to have a life of prayer. Likewise, love is not merely an event; love is an action. Thus, love is a language and life. Not only does Amanda write about love with a holy passion, but her life exemplifies the same. Her writing is a testament to everything the Lord has placed inside her. The words on every page are not just the sage words of a woman who has lived this life, but they are her gift and her grace.

Far more than a motivational book, When Love Pours, Love Speaks is a daily devotional from which you will feast on daily bread and draw from the glory of God. As you delve into this book of love, you will discover the heart of a woman of God with a revelation of the Father and the Father's love that is second to none. Read this book knowing that the author has already fulfilled John 13:35: "By this shall all men know that you are My disciples, if you have love for one another." Yes, all men know; those of us who have had the pleasure of sitting under her ministry know.

Those who know and love Amanda have experienced Love that Pours because when you are in the presence of Amanda, Love Speaks. Prepare for a life-changing experience as you turn every page; let love pour, and let love speak.

Apostle Clayton D. Smith

Pastor, Bread of Life Church,

Albany, Georgia/Birmingham, Alabama
Author of Amazon Bestseller Beyond the Palace:
The Implications of Joseph's Dreams

"
    Faith has perfected my hope, and love is my eternal reassurance.

————————————————

"
Our freedom to choose is an expression of God's love.

_____

- TABLE OF CONTENT -

- ENDORSEMENTS - III

- DEDICATION - V

- SCRIPTURES - VI

- FOREWORD - VII

JANUARY 1

FEBRUARY 13

MARCH 25

APRIL..39

MAY 51

JUNE...63

JULY 77

AUGUST 89

SEPTEMBER 103

OCTOBER 115

NOVEMBER...129

DECEMBER...141

- ABOUT THE AUTHOR - 155

WHEN LOVE POURS, LOVE Speaks

DAILY DEVOTION

January

JANUARY: DAY ~ 1

"

It is good to owe no man anything but love.

_____

JANUARY: DAY ~ 2

"

God's love was demonstrated in the giving of His dear Son as a ransom for all humanity.

_____

JANUARY: DAY ~ 3

"

Love made a way and became the way, the truth, and the life.

JANUARY: DAY ~ 4

" When I see red roses, I see whispers of God's love that runs red.

_____

JANUARY: DAY ~ 5

" God's love for us needs no occasion; every day is a love day.

_____

JANUARY: DAY ~ 6

" Beloved, our God has placed us on a love journey so that we might see and know His divine illumination and habitation in us.

JANUARY: DAY ~ 7

"
    Those who fall in love with love can easily fall out with it. Love is more than a feeling; love is also a choice.

————————————————

JANUARY: DAY ~ 8

"
    Our prayers don't have to be audible to be heard by God. His ears can hear hearts.

————————————————

JANUARY: DAY ~ 9

"
    Beauty comes in all shades, shapes, and sizes. Love the skin you are in; it's yours!

JANUARY: DAY ~ 10

"
It is good to be loved and to give love. God is love; we are all made in His image and likeness.

_____

JANUARY: DAY ~ 11

"
Love lifted me, and now I am seated in Heavenly Places!

_____

JANUARY: DAY ~ 12

"
Beloved, death gives no heartache that the Lord can't heal. Love gives memories no one can steal.

JANUARY: DAY ~ 13

"
Real love is not pretentious; it is profound!

_____

JANUARY: DAY ~ 14

"
Being in Christ is receiving beauty for ashes, salvation with benefits, a garment of praise for heaviness, a love that can't be denied, and a hope and a future that is eternal.

_____

JANUARY: DAY ~ 15

"
When we stray away, and our life seems to be in disarray, His wondrous love remains stable, for it is everlasting.

JANUARY: DAY ~ 16

"
Death cannot conquer love;
love is stronger.

_____

JANUARY: DAY ~ 17

"
If we are debtors to others, let it only be
for love.

_____

JANUARY: DAY ~ 18

"
A heart that knows love is a heart that
can give love.

JANUARY: DAY ~ **19**

" His love is never-ending, and so is His amazing grace.

———————————————

JANUARY: DAY ~ **20**

" Love's significance can be seen in a heart of faithful and willing obedience.

———————————————

JANUARY: DAY ~ **21**

" When we are too busy to receive or give love, we are too busy.

JANUARY: DAY ~ 22

"
    Love never works hard to convince us of its goodness; love seeks no reputation of its own. Goodness is the fruit of His love.

——————————————

JANUARY: DAY ~ 23

"
    God's love doesn't compete or compel. His love completes and consumes.

——————————————

JANUARY: DAY ~ 24

"
    Loving out loud isn't a duty; it is a desire.

9

JANUARY: DAY ~ **25**

"
It's easy to see how the Father truly loves us; it is etched on the face of every smile.

JANUARY: DAY ~ **26**

"
Love doesn't tear us down—love lifts us up.

JANUARY: DAY ~ **27**

"
Beloved, as the sunshine creates a brilliant tapestry of radiating light, so does the Father's love upon the canvas of our hearts. His love never fails.

JANUARY: DAY ~ 28

"
I am finding His joy in my journey because He loves me with passion.

_____

JANUARY: DAY ~ 29

"
We are all dirt and come in an array of loving colors. No matter the color of our dirt, we all became a living soul when the breath of God gave us life. We are all made in the image and likeness of His amazing love.

_____

JANUARY: DAY ~ 30

"
Love sees no color.

"
    The desire for love can possess a treasure full of truth. Some truths are released with time, and some are instinctively and quietly conveyed.

Be still my soul, for I need to hear far more than what my flesh is saying to me. Abba Father, thank You for speaking to my heart and revealing to me the truth of Your love and perfect will.

February

FEBRUARY: DAY ~ 1

" Love's compassion is the cure for cruelty.

_____

FEBUARY: DAY ~ 2

" When we love out loud, it can be seen in our giving.

_____

FEBUARY: DAY ~ 3

" To see no evil, to hear no evil, to speak no evil is to embrace a pure heart.

FEBUARY: DAY ~ 4

" Fear flees in the face of perfect love.

_____

FEBUARY: DAY ~ 5

" Love knows how to bear good fruit.

_____

FEBUARY: DAY ~ 6

" Speak love; it's a language everybody understands.

FEBUARY: DAY ~ 7

"
Love's motive is revealed by its character.

———————————————

FEBUARY: DAY ~ 8

"
Love is a gift that keeps on giving.

———————————————

FEBUARY: DAY ~ 9

"
Love is a good investment that can yield forth sustainable riches.

FEBUARY: DAY ~ 10

"
    Our Father's love is Extraordinary,

Enduring, Endearing, Exciting, Everlasting, Expansive, Expressive, Excellent, Encouraging, Enjoyable, Enormous, Extravagant, Exquisite, Endless, Ecstatic, Enlightening, Enormous, Essential, Empowering, Eternal!

_____

FEBUARY: DAY ~ 11

"
    Love has no substitutes because there is no equal.

_____

FEBUARY: DAY ~ 12

"
    The best in humanity is found in how we love one another.

FEBUARY: DAY ~ **13**

"
When we become intentional in loving others, there will be no room for hate.

_____

FEBUARY: DAY ~ **14**

"
Love has a need—and you are it!

_____

FEBUARY: DAY ~ **15**

"
Beloved, a heart that loves God doesn't operate in strife, bickering, and malice. A heart that loves God operates in love, truth, and obedience. Father, show us Your will and Your way that we may walk therein.

FEBUARY: DAY ~ 16

"
　　When our main focus is love, hate will cease to cloud our judgment or hijack our motives.

_____

FEBUARY: DAY ~ 17

"
　　The Father's love enables us to give with our expectations upon Him.

_____

FEBUARY: DAY ~ 18

"
　　The beauty of love can be seen in redemption.

FEBUARY: DAY ~ 19

"
    Love sees no difference in oneness; we are all made the same.

_____

FEBUARY: DAY ~ 20

"
    Love has a purpose—and it is you!

_____

FEBUARY: DAY ~ 21

"
    When we are blinded by hate, we can't recognize love.

FEBUARY: DAY ~ 22

"
True love is not governed; it is given.

FEBUARY: DAY ~ 23

"
Love is like a bridge; it carries and supports.

FEBUARY: DAY ~ 24

"
Take the limits off; in the sea of His love, there is no drowning.

FEBUARY: DAY ~ 25

"
The world seeks for personality, ambition, and charm, but the Father is after the heart.

_____

FEBUARY: DAY ~ 26

"
Love sees beyond the color of the skin into the very heart and soul.

_____

FEBUARY: DAY ~ 27

"
Love is not an accident waiting to happen. Love is a cure-all, ready to save, heal, and restore.

"

What's love got to do with it?

Everything!!!
Jesus' love paid it all, and His love ended it all!

One Offering
One Sacrifice
One New Man—Jew and Gentile!

For God so loved the world that He gave His only begotten Son that whosoever believeth in Him should not perish, but have everlasting life (John 3:16).

Beloved, love not only made a way; love became The Way!

WHEN LOVE
POURS,
LOVE
Speaks

DAILY DEVOTION

March

MARCH: DAY ~ 1

"
When others hate us without a cause, we can still choose to love them on purpose.

_____

MARCH: DAY ~ 2

"
We don't have to be perfect to receive the Father's love. His love perfects us.

_____

MARCH: DAY ~ 3

"
Beauty may fade, but the beauty of a loving heart is unforgettable.

MARCH: DAY ~ 4

"
   Life is a story of hope, triumph, loss, love, pain, sunshine, joy, heartache, and healing rain.

_____

MARCH: DAY ~ 5

"
   His love has favorites—and we all qualify.

_____

MARCH: DAY ~ 6

"
   When those who love us push too hard, it may seem like they want us to fall, but they know we are ready to fly.

MARCH: DAY ~ 7

" Love does not take advantage but gives in abundance.

MARCH: DAY ~ 8

" Love is a gift given to be received. Hate is a mindset that is taught to believe.

MARCH: DAY ~ 9

" If your love feels burdened, remember, all things were fulfilled when His love ran red.

MARCH: DAY ~ 10

" Love is the teacher, and we are all pupils.

―――――――――――――――

MARCH: DAY ~ 11

" Those things we hate, we can easily become, and those things we love can easily be won.

―――――――――――――――

MARCH: DAY ~ 12

" He who flaunts a cheating heart is truly destitute of real love.

MARCH: DAY ~ **13**

"
Love is stronger than death because death was conquered by love.

_____

MARCH: DAY ~ **14**

"
Love does not make excuses—love makes amends.

_____

MARCH: DAY ~ **15**

"
Love's simplicity can speak to hate's dominance.

MARCH: DAY ~ 16

"
Shared hope is one of love's shared joys.

_____

MARCH: DAY ~ 17

"
Love has no magic, only hearts that know love never fails.

_____

MARCH: DAY ~ 18

"
Love has a memory that never fades; it captures the heart and is stronger than any blade.

MARCH: DAY ~ **19**

" Love never punishes us for mistakes because it knows we are becoming fully awake.

_____

MARCH: DAY ~ **20**

" We can never repay the gift of His love, but we can give Him ourselves.

_____

MARCH: DAY ~ **21**

" True love will not cause us to bury who we are, but allow us to grow and blossom.

MARCH: DAY ~ 22

"
    A heart ignited by evil can be a changed heart ignited by love!

MARCH: DAY ~ 23

"
    Love paid the price and became the ultimate sacrifice.

MARCH: DAY ~ 24

"
    All things are pure to those whose hearts are matured in love.

MARCH: DAY ~ 25

" Love was nailed to a cross for you and me that we would no longer be blind but healed and set free!

MARCH: DAY ~ 26

" The Son of Man is the perfect portrait of the Father's love.

MARCH: DAY ~ 27

" Love is never stumbled upon, for its path is always divinely directed.

MARCH: DAY ~ 28

"
When love labors, its purpose isn't to be seen but to heal, restore, and esteem.

_____

MARCH: DAY ~ 29

"
His love assures us even when we lose confidence in ourselves and others.

_____

MARCH: DAY ~ 30

"
The innocence of love never wavers, for its nature always remains the same.

MARCH: DAY ~ 31

"
DANCE WITH ME

Have you ever noticed that many ballroom dancers who are competitors become emotionally and physically connected? During the process of practicing hours and hours and spending a lot of time together, chemistry is formed, and the passion between the two can be felt and demonstrated in their dance!

Beloved, when we dance with Yeshua, the true lover of our soul, the intensity of His great LOVE and PASSION becomes infused within us! Yeshua is Lord of the Dance, and He is WOOING us to dance a dance with Him that is sure to ravish our SPIRIT, SOUL, and BODY! I love watching how the male dancer leads, and the female responds in total harmony with such precision, poise, and rhythm to his every move! Developing these

skills takes years of practice, commitment, dedication, and the RIGHT PARTNER in professional dancing!

Beloved, we have the PERFECT PARTNER, and He is waiting to LEAD us in a dance of INTIMACY and DELIGHT that REVEALS His true HEART and PASSION for us! I can picture Yeshua dressed in royal attire, flowing gracefully with His dazzling bride in a romantic Waltz! Each step is harmonically synchronized, and both are locked in a romantic embrace destined to last for ALL ETERNITY!

I love the song:

> Behold, You have come over the hills, upon the mountains
> To me, You have run
> My Beloved, You've captured my heart....
> Won't You dance with me
> Oh, Lover of my soul
> To the song of all songs?...
> Romance me
> Oh, Lover of my soul
> To the song of all songs.
> (Song by Jesus Culture)

The Word tells us: He will rejoice over us with joy! He will calm us in His love! He will rejoice over us with singing (Zephaniah 3:17 WEB).

Beloved, as His dear bride, may our hearts begin to desire and seek moments alone with the Lover of our soul!

May we stand IN AWE daily with much excitement and anticipation of each lesson and each dance, His loving embrace and gentle touch, and the joyful sound of our Bridegroom singing over us!

LET'S DANCE!!!

April

APRIL: DAY ~ 1

"
Love never sleeps; its watchful gaze is upon us all.

_____

APRIL: DAY ~ 2

"
Love never fails, even when we fail to love.

_____

APRIL: DAY ~ 3

"
Where there is injustice, there is compassion.
Where there is compassion, there is love.
Where there is love, there is hope.
Where there is hope, there is the Light of Glory that brings forth transformation!

APRIL: DAY ~ 4

" In the stillness of love's peace, fear has no home.

————————

APRIL: DAY ~ 5

" Beloved, our Father has caused all humanity to soar with the Son. To rise above all obstacles, declaring His mercy and truth are met together, that righteousness and peace have kissed each other, and that we are made as One! To see every wave of adversity as prayers already answered. To fly beneath the heavens under the canopy of His warm embrace, forever free, forever immersed in His passionate and faithful love, Soaring!

APRIL: DAY ~ 6

"
Don't allow heartache to rule—but allow love to heal.

_____

APRIL: DAY ~ 7

"
A sharing heart is a gift of love.

_____

APRIL: DAY ~ 8

"
Worship that is forced is manipulated. Worship birthed out of desire is the motive of love.

APRIL: DAY ~ 9

"
Love loves all races because love sees through one blood.

APRIL: DAY ~ 10

"
Love expressed is love lived!

APRIL: DAY ~ 11

"
Love breeds contentment and not contention.

APRIL: DAY ~ 12

" Love is simple, especially when it's expressed through a willing heart.

APRIL: DAY ~ 13

" Love can build a strong foundation that is sure to stand.

APRIL: DAY ~ 14

" When we allow love to discipline us, we can become love's disciples.

APRIL: DAY ~ 15

"
A pretentious love will always bring up our mistakes, but a faithful love will love us through them all.

_____

APRIL: DAY ~ 16

"
Love is the greatest key that connects us together.

_____

APRIL: DAY ~ 17

"
Love can be comforted by truth because love knows they are allies.

APRIL: DAY ~ **18**

"
Home is where the heart is, especially when that home is a space conducive to love.

_____

APRIL: DAY ~ **19**

"
In looking for love in all the wrong places, we can overlook the right place that matters the most—yourself.

_____

APRIL: DAY ~ **20**

"
There is no substitute for God's love, only counterfeits.

APRIL: DAY ~ **21**

"

    When love offered up a sacrifice, we were always part of the plan.

_____

APRIL: DAY ~ **22**

"

    Love is not magical—love is DIVINE!

_____

APRIL: DAY ~ **23**

"

    We all can be teachers of love as we become love's example.

APRIL: DAY ~ 24

"
Thank You, Abba

Thank You, Abba, for helping me cast off
  every weight.
To trust You, Abba, in every step that I take.
To look to You as the Author and the
  Finisher of my faith,
To know I have the belt of truth fastened
  around my waist.
To stay firmly encouraged in You through all
  kinds of storms.
To know that You always have my back in
  whatever may be formed.
To receive my help that comes daily from
  You,
To acknowledge You in all my ways, in all I
say and do.
To know even in my pain, You are well
  acquainted with my grief,
To receive Your hope even in my times of
  unbelief.
Thank You, Abba, for speaking peace to my
  soul.
And thank You for allowing me each day
  to experience the greatest love story
  ever told!

APRIL: DAY ~ 25

"
The beauty of love is mirrored in those who can see its true reflection.

APRIL: DAY ~ 26

"
Father, Your love declares that I am enough.

APRIL: DAY ~ 27

"
Love is never hidden, but sometimes it can be disguised and revealed to the prudent, the meek, and the wise.

APRIL: DAY ~ **28**

"
Love spoke through pain on the cross and allowed us all to be restored and not remain lost

_____

APRIL: DAY ~ **29**

"
A child who is taught how to hate can grow up to experience how to love.

_____

APRIL: DAY ~ **30**

"
Love poured out is love that can be poured in.

May

MAY: DAY ~ 1

“
Beloved, perfect love perfects sons!

—————————————

MAY: DAY ~ 2

“
Love never reminds us of our failures because love never forgets our potential.

—————————————

MAY: DAY ~ 3

“
When love becomes the language we teach, it can be heard in the words that we speak.

MAY: DAY ~ 4

"
His love chose me even when I didn't choose love.

_____

MAY: DAY ~ 5

"
When we lose ourselves to be loved by others, finding ourselves will be of the utmost importance.

_____

MAY: DAY ~ 6

"
Love never teaches us how to hate, but those who hate can be shown how to love.

MAY: DAY ~ 7

"
Love and kindness always have the power to heal.

MAY: DAY ~ 8

"
When we believe we need a reason to love, look at the man in the mirror.

MAY: DAY ~ 9

"
Hope is not lost in love—it is found.

MAY: DAY ~ 10

"
When we speak the truth in love, those who are listening will be able to hear what we say.

_____

MAY: DAY ~ 11

"
Love can turn a frown into a smile.

_____

MAY: DAY ~ 12

"
The love of Christ can be graciously shown when we can love strongly those who have done us wrong.

MAY: DAY ~ 13

"
    A price many pay to be loved isn't a debt they owe. True love freely gives.

_____

MAY: DAY ~ 14

"
    The gift of the Father's love is not measured by our mistakes. His love is unconditional.

_____

MAY: DAY ~ 15

"
    His love forever completes me, not the opinions of others.

MAY: DAY ~ 16

"
Love never compares. Love completes!

————————————

MAY: DAY ~ 17

"
Love is a novice when it involves hate.

————————————

MAY: DAY ~ 18

"
Loving yourself is an essential ingredient in dealing with self-worth.

MAY: DAY ~ 19

" Love's fruit is eternal—it never spoils.

MAY: DAY ~ 20

" Fragile is the heart full of hate because it is destitute of love.

MAY: DAY ~ 21

" Love has a distinct sound that can be heard in any language.

MAY: DAY ~ 22

"
When love is being judged, its greatest defense will always be love.

---

MAY: DAY ~ 23

"
Love does not make us its slaves, for a true heart of love isn't afraid of commitment.

MAY: DAY ~ 24

"
True love is worth the wait, especially when you know you're not waiting alone.

MAY: DAY ~ 25

" Nothing speaks love like a giving heart.

——————————————

MAY: DAY ~ 26

" Love never takes; it always gives more, especially of itself.

——————————————

MAY: DAY ~ 27

" When people love you for who you are, they won't be concerned about who you are not.

MAY: DAY ~ 28

"
True love never dies, but hate always has a death sentence.

_____

MAY: DAY ~ 29

"
The Father's love is available to carry us even when we fall behind.

_____

MAY: DAY ~ 30

"
Love never looks for a reason to be obedient.

MAY: DAY ~ 31

"

Give Me My Flowers

Give me my flowers, while I live,
Let me gaze upon their beauty and inhale
the fragrance of Nature's jewels.
Give me my flowers, so I can see the glory
of each color,
And adorn my surroundings with a palette of
amazing hues.

Give me my flowers, so I can reminisce in
the glow of the morning light as each bloom
beckons for my undivided attention.
Give me my flowers, so I may sit and
contemplate on the magnificent pleasures,
Mesmerized by life radiating from every
lovely petal.

Give me my flowers, so I can hold them with
a gentle hug, quietly captured by a bouquet
of scented lullabies.
Give me my flowers, while my blood is still
running warm within my veins, as my heart
still beats, and all my senses are fully
engaged.

Give me my flowers, whatever they may be,
so that I can experience and reminisce on
the sweetness of my Father's love, one
breath at a time!

June

JUNE: DAY ~ 1

" Love doesn't care about the mistakes you made because it always remembers the debt has already been fully paid.

———————————————

JUNE: DAY ~ 2

" Love always gives us a second chance; if you need more, don't worry, love is not keeping tabs.

———————————————

JUNE: DAY ~ 3

" Forgiveness can be heard when the mouth speaks from a heart filled with love.

JUNE: DAY ~ 4

"

When we learn how to truly love, when it is tested, we will pass.

_____

JUNE: DAY ~ 5

"

Our Father's love was never left up to chance. When breath was breathed into Adam, love was inhaled by us all!

_____

JUNE: DAY ~ 6

"

Beloved, the older we get, the more we can enjoy the privileges of what we have learned of our Father's love that never fails.

JUNE: DAY ~ 7

"
    When we allow the shelter of love to be a habitat, those who enter in will know that love is where the heart is.

_____

JUNE: DAY ~ 8

"
    Love came down, love lived amongst us, love died, love rose, and love became our all in all!

_____

JUNE: DAY ~ 9

"
    Love said He would, and love graciously did!

JUNE: DAY ~ 10

"
    In a place of weakness, you can find
Strength.
In place of hate, you can embrace Love.
In a place of loneliness, you can receive
  Consolation.
In a place of confusion, you can obtain
  Peace.
In a place of ridicule, you can know Truth.
In a place of lack, you can be Restored.
In a place of darkness, you have been given
Eternal Light!

JUNE: DAY ~ 11

"
    Love is our greatest teacher, especially
when we are ready to learn.

JUNE: DAY ~ 12

"
When hate from others comes your way, trust that love has already saved the day.

_____

JUNE: DAY ~ 13

"
The beauty of love can be measured by a heart that willingly forgives.

_____

JUNE: DAY ~ 14

"
If love had a secret, it would be that it's intentional.

JUNE: DAY ~ 15

"
   When we walk by faith, we will discover that it works by love.

_____

JUNE: DAY ~ 16

"
   When love tames a savage beast, the heart is never the same.

_____

JUNE: DAY ~ 17

"
   Love is not our task master; love is our home!

JUNE: DAY ~ 18

"
When you find someone who can love you for who you are, no need to pretend to be someone you are not.

JUNE: DAY ~ 19

"
When true discernment is empowered by love, it can bear no false witness.

JUNE: DAY ~ 20

"
Love makes a deposit that vastly accumulates into riches.

JUNE: DAY ~ **21**

"
Sweet is the taste of His love that causes our hearts to partake daily.

JUNE: DAY ~ **22**

"
Love is incapable of dying, but hate demands to be kept alive.

JUNE: DAY ~ **23**

"
Love stands us up to walk in His footsteps.

JUNE: DAY ~ 24

"
Peace is a fruit of love that is steadfast and constant.

_____

JUNE: DAY ~ 25

"
Love inspires, Hope endures, and Faith believes!

_____

JUNE: DAY ~ 26

"
Some things are meant to be kept and never shared, but I am sure love isn't one of them.

JUNE: DAY ~ 27

"
When we practice loving ourselves, we can know how to love others.

_____

JUNE: DAY ~ 28

"
Love spelled backwards is EVOL,

the first four letters of evolution. In the beginning, God's love created the heavens and the earth.

_____

JUNE: DAY ~ 29

"
Love never holds a grudge; love holds forgiveness. The greatest acts of love can be seen in a selfless heart.

JUNE: DAY ~ **30**

"

His Bride Faithfully Intercedes

We draw near in true intimacy. As our personal encounters are rekindled and renewed, You are touching our hearts with Your passion to love and to serve!

Come, and upon our hearts awaken us to Your truth,
truth that will touch nations with Your wondrous love, peace, signs, and wonders to see and experience Your holy habitation!

Come in us as the bright and morning star, appearing in all our now to establish Your Kingdom and change our entire earth with Your glory!

We declare that we are Your beloved bride, and You are the resting place in our hearts!

The kisses of Your mouth, Your words are sweet, and Your love is better than fine wine!

The fragrance of Your extravagant love is intoxicating, and it is

74

ravishing our hearts in a flame of fire to come deeper still! We hear You knocking upon the door of our hearts, and we say:

You are welcome in this place!

Forever You are Mine, and forever we are Yours.

Enter in!

WHEN LOVE POURS, LOVE Speaks

DAILY DEVOTION

July

JULY: DAY ~ 1

" Love has the power to create, heal, and restore.

_____

JULY: DAY ~ 2

" If your love needs a reason to love, it's not the real thing!

_____

JULY: DAY ~ 3

" You can love what you do when you are doing what you love.

JULY: DAY ~ 4

"
When we start to love ourselves, it can create a path to inner healing.

———————————————

JULY: DAY ~ 5

"
Love became the sacrifice, and we are the eternal recipients.

———————————————

JULY: DAY ~ 6

"
There is no statute of limitation upon love, according to love.

JULY: DAY ~ 7

" The true nature of kindness is respect and love.

JULY: DAY ~ 8

" The Father's love is indescribable, but in His Son, love is fully made known!

JULY: DAY ~ 9

" Never fall out of love with yourself because you will always have you.

JULY: DAY ~ 10

" To know love is to be acquainted with it.

_____

JULY: DAY ~ 11

" When you grow old in love, you realize that true love is ageless!

_____

JULY: DAY ~ 12

" Love has a distinct sound that can be heard in joy, peace, long-suffering, gentleness, goodness, faith, meekness, and temperance.

JULY: DAY ~ **13**

"
No reason is needed to love, only a heart to obey.

_____

JULY: DAY ~ **14**

"
Beloved, His love is the Home where our hearts can find absolute rest.

_____

JULY: DAY ~ **15**

"
The power of forgiveness affords us to love and live!

JULY: DAY ~ 16

"
Love never fails because there is no failure in God.

JULY: DAY ~ 17

"
True love converts, comforts, and completes. Love doesn't try to control, constrict, or constrain.

JULY: DAY ~ 18

"
Beloved, kindness is a fruit derived from the essence of love.

JULY: DAY ~ 19

" Love demonstrated is love in action!

JULY: DAY ~ 20

" There is strength in abiding in the peace of His sustaining love.

JULY: DAY ~ 21

" Love the skin that you are in; you are the only one wearing the real package, and no duplicates were made.

JULY: DAY ~ **22**

"
   When we are taught how to love, we can learn not to hate.

_____

JULY: DAY ~ **23**

"
   The love of God doesn't take us by force; His love graciously woos us.

_____

JULY: DAY ~ **24**

"
   A snapshot can capture a glimpse in time, but perfect love is always eternal and divine.

JULY: DAY ~ 25

"
When love gives us an assignment, it will not be anything that we can't accomplish.

_____

JULY: DAY ~ 26

"
Those we outgrow are not those we step on. True maturity resonates with peace and genuine love.

_____

JULY: DAY ~ 27

"
Love has wings, and they are able to stretch forth and carry us all.

JULY: DAY ~ **28**

"
Beauty can beckon our heart to draw near, but love allows our heart to stay.

JULY: DAY ~ **29**

"
The sound of love can be heard when we become love's instrument.

JULY: DAY ~ **30**

"
Love finds a way even when the journey seems impossible.

JULY: DAY ~ 31

"
   My Latter Years

My latter years shall be my best years,
For the Refiner has so decreed,
In His hands, I am fashioned
Wrought from an eternal seed.

Captured by His love
And pursued along my course,
His gaze is always upon me,
He has always been my source.
To see Him face to face,
Drawn sweetly to His Throne,
My life reflects His goodness
In all that He has shown.

Each day, I receive new mercy
To boldly draw near,
To know that I am seated,
Where there is no fear.

My latter years shall be my best years,
For I am fearfully and wondrously made.
My life is not my own,
And upon me, His righteousness is
beautifully displayed.

August

AUGUST: DAY ~ 1

" Fear is no match for perfect love.

_____

AUGUST: DAY ~ 2

" Love is relevant to those who are willing to trust and obey.

_____

AUGUST: DAY ~ 3

" A thankful heart knows the wealth of love among friends.

AUGUST: DAY ~ 4

"
Love can cause two hearts to beat as one, for they become one.

―――――――――――――

AUGUST: DAY ~ 5

"
Perfect love knows the value of trust and knows how to maintain its treasure.

―――――――――――――

AUGUST: DAY ~ 6

"
Goodness and kindness are never far away from love.

AUGUST: DAY ~ 7

"
Love is our hope in the midst of any uncertainty.

—————————————

AUGUST: DAY ~ 8

"
Beloved, love is never absent from a heart that can receive it.

—————————————

AUGUST: DAY ~ 9

"
Love is eternal; love speaks to everything and to everyone!

AUGUST: DAY ~ **10**

"
His love is able to conquer all our fears.

_____

AUGUST: DAY ~ **11**

"
Love recognizes us even in the dark and provides comfort and protection.

_____

AUGUST: DAY ~ **12**

"
Love's sweet melody sounds in
a heart that knows it's an instrument.

AUGUST: DAY ~ 13

"
The simplicity of love is revealed in love's strength.

_____

AUGUST: DAY ~ 14

"
He saw me lonely, broken, naked, and afraid. His amazing love sweetly embraces and divinely arrays!

_____

AUGUST: DAY ~ 15

"
The testimony of the Father's love never wavers, denies, forsakes, or forgets.
His love is faithful and seeks to pardon.

AUGUST: DAY ~ **16**

"

Love knows how to speak to pain even in times of silent numbness.

AUGUST: DAY ~ **17**

"

Love has a fragrance all of its own; a sweet aroma that can be experienced and known.

AUGUST: DAY ~ **18**

"

The love of our Father was shown in the giving of His Son, and every day we can experience His love and all that He has done.

AUGUST: DAY ~ 19

"
    True love has no motive other than to love.

_____

AUGUST: DAY ~ 20

"
    Love sees us for who we really are and not who we are ashamed to be.

_____

AUGUST: DAY ~ 21

"
    Love can be gifted in many ways, but the giving of ourselves is the most important of them all.

AUGUST: DAY ~ 22

"
   Those who try to run from the Father's love run right into it because it's inescapable!

_____

AUGUST: DAY ~ 23

"
   A fool in love can be awakened to a love that does not fool.

_____

AUGUST: DAY ~ 24

"
   When truth is filtered through love, the matters of the heart can be revealed to heal.

AUGUST: DAY ~ 25

"
Love doesn't shame or expose; love covers even those things we don't think it knows.

_____

AUGUST: DAY ~ 26

"
Hate is good at making withdrawals, but love is always invested in making deposits.

_____

AUGUST: DAY ~ 27

"
Many spend years looking for love and have failed to see that love has been there all the time.

AUGUST: DAY ~ **28**

"
Love isn't a strong arm over us; love holds us strong!

AUGUST: DAY ~ **29**

"
Love will always foster the truth and be its keeper.

AUGUST: DAY ~ **30**

"
His love speaks peace to our soul.
For in Him, we are made completely whole!

AUGUST: DAY ~ 31

"

Jesus, The Fragrant One

Because of the savor and smell of Your good ointments, Your name is as ointment poured forth, therefore do the virgins love thee (Song of Solomon 1:3).

In reading this scripture, I can see the symbolic nature of our Lord reflected in the story of the Alabaster Box.
His Name is like ointment poured forth, and it flows from the fragrance of His Goodness, His love, His nature, His character, His reputation!
His fragrance is refreshing, soothing, and comforting, exuding a pleasant and sweet aroma that's eternal.

The Alabaster box is a beautiful representation of the body of our Lord. He was housed in an earthly vessel and became "The Fragrance" poured out for us all. The savor of good ointments poured upon all mankind!

At Bethany, His response to those who replied, "Why was this ointment wasted, for it could have been sold for much more?
"This was done for my burial."
Jesus was and is the precious perfume

poured out;
His flesh was broken to release the precious
ointment that saves, heals, restores, renews,
and refreshes!

May we receive the balm, the ointment of
Gilead, and inhale the refreshing fragrance
of His divine nature extravagantly poured out
upon us all.

The fragrance of our Lord fills our temples
and saturates us with a sweet-smelling
perfume!

Hallelujah!

Father, we thank You for the sweet, savor
fragrance of Your Son, who poured upon us
Himself, as Your divine ointment who heals,
restores, and revives!

May we inhale and exhale all that Jesus is,
in Truth and in Spirit.
May we continually know that the banner
over us is His extravagant love and
sweet-sweet perfume!

May we know that we
are His garden enclosed
to bring forth precious
fruits planted by Living Waters!

We declare the winds of His truth

are blowing upon His garden and the
sweetness of His aroma flows upon all our
earth. All His pleasant fruits are yielding forth
life and life more abundantly.

We saturate in His presence and His
fragrance permeates our entire being!
We come, reflecting upon His redeeming
love, knowing we are indeed eternal heirs
of His divine exchange, the essence of His
anointed fragrance!

Amen.

September

SEPTEMBER: DAY ~ 1

"
    Love said, "I will be the sacrifice!" Love said, "It is finished!" Love said, "I will return, and for all eternity, I am Yours and you are mine!"

_____

SEPTEMBER: DAY ~ 2

"
    Love people where they are and trust God to bring them where they need to be.

_____

SEPTEMBER: DAY ~ 3

"
    The Father's love is always exciting, and He beckons us to come, for He delights in inviting.

SEPTEMBER: DAY ~ 4

" Those who are led by love are easily acquainted with love.

_____

SEPTEMBER: DAY ~ 5

" Sin carried an ultimate penalty, but His love paid the ultimate price.

_____

SEPTEMBER: DAY ~ 6

" All hearts were made for love and to love.

SEPTEMBER: DAY ~ 7

"
Love is audible in compassion.

SEPTEMBER: DAY ~ 8

"
When we see with the eyes of love, love responds.

SEPTEMBER: DAY ~ 9

"
Hate is treatable; the cure is love.

SEPTEMBER: DAY ~ 10

"
A voice of righteous indignation loves repentance.

SEPTEMBER: DAY ~ 11

"
In the fall of man, death screamed, "Yes," but love declared, "No!"

SEPTEMBER: DAY ~ 12

"
Hope has a destination, and it is Eternal Love!

SEPTEMBER: DAY ~ **13**

"
Through difficult situations, we can learn to mature in love.

_____

SEPTEMBER: DAY ~ **14**

"
Love allows us to see who we were meant to be.

_____

SEPTEMBER: DAY ~ **15**

"
To be our brother's keeper is to love as we love ourselves.

SEPTEMBER: DAY ~ **16**

"
Perfect love loves without conditions, for it is unconditional.

_____

SEPTEMBER: DAY ~ **17**

"
Love is more than an experience, love is Eternal!

_____

SEPTEMBER: DAY ~ **18**

"
Love can be expressed in any language and heard by those who desperately need it.

SEPTEMBER: DAY ~ 19

"
   Abba Father

Abba Father, thanks for being a loving
Father who made me just like You.
A Father who is always present, so faithful,
and forever true.

You are the total essence of my life, the
beginning of my being,
The One who holds me close, the
completeness of my ending.

You knew my name way before I was
conceived,
You crowned me with lovingkindness, and
eternal heritage I have received!

Thanks for being my Father who always
knows best,

The One who loves me for all eternity and
has secured me in Your absolute Rest!

SEPTEMBER: DAY ~ **20**

"
    Love your silver strands, they love you.
That's why they fight to stay around.

SEPTEMBER: DAY ~ **21**

"
    The beauty of His love knows no
ugliness.

SEPTEMBER: DAY ~ **22**

"
    Love does not attract evil; love consumes
it!

SEPTEMBER: DAY ~ 23

"
Love matters, no matter what the condition we see the world in.

_____

SEPTEMBER: DAY ~ 24

"
Look into the mirror of His word and know that you are love's Eternal Reality!

_____

SEPTEMBER: DAY ~ 25

"
The cost of His love was extravagant because He knew we were worth a King's ransom!

SEPTEMBER: DAY ~ 26

"
The answer to hatred is not hatred, the answer is love.

———————————————

SEPTEMBER: DAY ~ 27

"
If we all love others as we love ourselves, no one would ever be mistreated.

———————————————

SEPTEMBER: DAY ~ 28

"
Beloved, it's easy to operate in peace when we operate in love.

SEPTEMBER: DAY ~ 29

"
The heart of a child is fertile ground for seeds of love. What are you sowing?

_____

SEPTEMBER: DAY ~ 30

"
Love might not always be visible to the natural eye, but love is recognizable by the heart.

October

OCTOBER: DAY ~ 1

"
   When our hearts are bowed in shame and pain, may we come to know His love that's present to sustain.

OCTOBER: DAY ~ 2

"
   Love is more powerful than fear, and perfect love is the remedy.

OCTOBER: DAY ~ 3

"
   Anger can provoke us to wrath, but love can provoke us to compassion.

OCTOBER: DAY ~ 4

"
He Is Love

Beloved, I can hear the Father's heart calling us to a love we have yet to embrace and know. A love that truly bears all, forgives all, a love for which we are willing to lay down our lives. In comparison to His love, our love is finite, selfish, shallow, impatient, and indifferent; it only gives when it is given, and it falls very short of loving others as we love ourselves. His love sees not what is portrayed nor considers what is given. His love is unconditional, unfailing, and stronger than death! How can we obtain this awesome love, walk in this love, or even fathom this kind of love?

Beloved, our heart is the key! It is the very ground upon which His love is cultivated and matured! He has put forth His love in us by the giving of the Holy Spirit! He is perfecting us in His love through the many things we allow Him to speak into and shine His light upon. First, it starts with receiving His love for ourselves, knowing, indeed, that we are worthy of His love, and allowing His love to make us whole! How can we love like the Father when we don't know His love? How can we share the love of the

Father when we don't know how to receive His love for ourselves?

All of us are on a love journey, and along every step of this journey, our Father allows us to see and experience His extravagant love! For HE is love! Love made us, and His love is maturing us as He is! Beloved, when I think about how He loves me, my heart wants to know Him even the more!

I want to wait in His presence and see Him face-to-face! His words are whispering: "Blessed are those that are pure in heart, for they shall see me." I thank Father for this love journey! He is pressing us all in and bringing forth the true nature of His great love within His house! His tabernacle, His Beloved!

His "love is patient, love is kind. It does not envy, it does not boast, it is not proud. It does not dishonor others, it is not self-seeking, it is not easily angered, it keeps no record of wrongs." His "love does not delight in evil but rejoices with the truth. It always protects, always trusts, always hopes, always perseveres." Beloved, His love never fails! (1Cor. 13:4-13).

Beloved, we are the apple of His eye!

OCTOBER: DAY ~ 5

"

To walk in His love is to be a doer of the Word.

_____

OCTOBER: DAY ~ 6

"

Love will always teach us how to love, not to hate.

_____

OCTOBER: DAY ~ 7

"

Faith all your faith in love.

OCTOBER: DAY ~ 8

"
May our life be a sermon of peace, hope, and love.

————————————————

OCTOBER: DAY ~ 9

"
True love doesn't covet. It covers.

————————————————

OCTOBER: DAY ~ 10

"
It's in the darkness of our pain that the light of His love diminishes all hurt, guilt, and shame.

OCTOBER: DAY ~ 11

"
    To be fruitful in love is to multiply love in abundance.

————————————————

OCTOBER: DAY ~ 12

"
    Father God, Your love is constant and reassuring. Your love is full of compassion and forever enduring.

————————————————

OCTOBER: DAY ~ 13

"
    There is no substitute for real love, even though the world may offer us many versions.

OCTOBER: DAY ~ **14**

"
Beloved, we are so loved, made by love, made in love, made with love, and made for love.

_____

OCTOBER: DAY ~ **15**

"
When our hearts are guided by love, we can bear the fruit of integrity.

_____

OCTOBER: DAY ~ **16**

"
Perfect love doesn't wait to give; it always gives from the abundance of eternal treasures.

OCTOBER: DAY ~ 17

"
His love never says, "Just get over it."
His love will always guide us through it.

_____

OCTOBER: DAY ~ 18

"
It is easy to dispel hate when we choose
to walk in love.

_____

OCTOBER: DAY ~ 19

"
No one can love us the way we can;
self-love isn't selfish.

OCTOBER: DAY ~ 20

"
Love cures and it's the best antidote against hate.

OCTOBER: DAY ~ 21

"
Love put to a ballad can be musically displayed, but love put to the heart is spiritually conveyed.

OCTOBER: DAY ~ 22

"
Love doesn't see color; love sees the heart.

OCTOBER: DAY ~ 23

"
Only with the Father's love can we love others as we love ourselves.

_____

OCTOBER: DAY ~ 24

"
Surround yourself with faith, humility, and obedience, for these are great agents of love.

_____

OCTOBER: DAY ~ 25

"
Peace strength abides in love.

OCTOBER: DAY ~ 26

" The fruit of humility is love.

_____

OCTOBER: DAY ~ 27

" Love is a beautiful flame that never fades.

_____

OCTOBER: DAY ~ 28

" The fruit of the Father's love is evident in His mature sons and daughters.

OCTOBER: DAY ~ **29**

"
 The beauty of perfect love never tarnishes because it is forever.

_____

OCTOBER: DAY ~ **30**

"
 The richest wealth is God's love; He never stops giving.

_____

OCTOBER: DAY ~ **31**

"
 It's easy to be inspired by love when we realize it begins with us.

WHEN LOVE POURS, LOVE Speaks

DAILY DEVOTION

November

NOVEMBER: DAY ~ 1

" Love can be spoken, but it is given when it is shown.

_____

NOVEMBER: DAY ~ 2

" When love comes with demands, we have yet to walk in its maturity.

_____

NOVEMBER: DAY ~ 3

" The truth allows us to have direct contact with an everlasting love that secures and seals.

NOVEMBER: DAY ~ 4

"
The heart wasn't made to be inferior to love, for it's a wonderful conductor.

NOVEMBER: DAY ~ 5

"
A heart that nourishes love can truly give love.

NOVEMBER: DAY ~ 6

"
Our life's commission is to love, and we are perfectly suited for it.

NOVEMBER: DAY ~ 7

" Choose love because Love first chose us.

_____

NOVEMBER: DAY ~ 8

" We don't have to excel in love to love.

_____

NOVEMBER: DAY ~ 9

" Hope is the heart and strength of love.

NOVEMBER: DAY ~ 10

"
    His love is a sweet symphony of peace that saturates our souls.

NOVEMBER: DAY ~ 11

"
    True love offers us a way in and a way out.

NOVEMBER: DAY ~ 12

"
    His love never invites us to go it alone; His love never fails.

"

Are We Living in the Times of Jesus'
Return?
Are we living in the times of Jesus' return?
Do we need to be mindful, alert, and
  concerned?
In all the chaos, can we see what's truly
  going on?
Have we received His gift of salvation that
  graciously atones?

In times of uncertainty, are we drawing near?
To commune in His presence, to be still and
  faithfully hear?

Abba Father, You are speaking to our hearts
so that we can fully know, You alone are
Sovereign, and You are running the show.
May our eyes be fixed on You, and not
caught up in the maze, but steadfast in Your
love, walking diligently in all Your ways.

NOVEMBER: DAY ~ 14

"
Love's truth is never hidden; we only need His eyes to see.

_____

NOVEMBER: DAY ~ 15

"
Love speaks truth to love, and truth speaks love to truth.

_____

NOVEMBER: DAY ~ 16

"
True beauty is a heart transformed by the Word!

NOVEMBER: DAY ~ 17

"
    We have a choice to criticize, but a greater duty to love.

_____

NOVEMBER: DAY ~ 18

"
    A radical love can yield forth a radical praise!

_____

NOVEMBER: DAY ~ 19

"
    A kind smile can warm the heart, and the gift of love can save the soul.

NOVEMBER: DAY ~ 20

"
Forgiveness is great medicine for the heart.

_____

NOVEMBER: DAY ~ 21

"
Love never takes a vacation, but its journey is bound to an eternal destination.

_____

NOVEMBER: DAY ~ 22

"
True love doesn't hold prisoners; it sets us free!

NOVEMBER: DAY ~ 23

" Love isn't a conquest, and it knows no defeat; love gives the utmost and doesn't retreat.

_____

NOVEMBER: DAY ~ 24

" True love always shows its true colors; it has nothing to hide.

_____

NOVEMBER: DAY ~ 25

" The Father's love specializes in the hearts of all men.

NOVEMBER: DAY ~ 26

" Love never sees us as worthless but eternally worthy!

_____

NOVEMBER: DAY ~ 27

" Faith works by love, and love possesses a lot of faith to walk in.

_____

NOVEMBER: DAY ~ 28

" When love speaks, joy responds!

NOVEMBER: DAY ~ **29**

"
    Receive hope in faith, but most of all, walk in love.

——————————————

NOVEMBER: DAY ~ **30**

"
    Perfect love always makes good on its promises.

December

DECEMBER: DAY ~ 1

" Those who aren't afraid of their fragility can humbly plant seeds of love in the midst of thorns.

DECEMBER: DAY ~ 2

" God's love is radiant because His light echoes upon it.

DECEMBER: DAY ~ 3

" Love never says you can't; love is the ability to say you can!

DECEMBER: DAY ~ 4

"
The truth and love are one and the same.

————————————————

DECEMBER: DAY ~ 5

"
Even in silence, His love speaks volumes of goodness and mercy.

————————————————

DECEMBER: DAY ~ 6

"
We don't achieve God's love; we receive it.

DECEMBER: DAY ~ 7

"
The fabric of His truth is woven in love.

DECEMBER: DAY ~ 8

"
Love has a truth that desires not to be hidden, to the heart it's revealed and never forbidden.

DECEMBER: DAY ~ 9

"
The truth whispers to the heart in the language of love.

DECEMBER: DAY ~ 10

"
The Father's love protects and preserves even those considered underserved.

DECEMBER: DAY ~ 11

"
Love always goes the distance, even if we take detours.

DECEMBER: DAY ~ 12

"
Love doesn't seek revenge; love offers mercy.

DECEMBER: DAY ~ **13**

"
Love has patience and is willing to listen.

DECEMBER: DAY ~ **14**

"
Love is an eternal force!

DECEMBER: DAY ~ **15**

"
Love never takes a vacation because love is always celebrating you.

DECEMBER: DAY ~ 16

"

   Let Me Be Tomorrow, You

Let me be tomorrow, you
To walk in your shoes as you do.
To know the hurt that has caused you great
   pain.
To see with your eyes those things that are so
   plain.
To give you rest as I hold your burdens,
To experience the things that you feel are
   certain.
Let me be tomorrow, you,
For to love myself it is to also love you.

DECEMBER: DAY ~ 17

"

   We don't need a license to love;
our heart is all that's required.

DECEMBER: DAY ~ 18

" To speak confidently of love's truth is to experience it.

_____

DECEMBER: DAY ~ 19

" A wandering heart seeks to give love a try. In the midst of uncertainty, true love becomes the reason why.

_____

DECEMBER: DAY ~ 20

" To be a steward of love is to see yourself as the recipient.

DECEMBER: DAY ~ 21

"
A smile is a visual vibration of love sounding.

DECEMBER: DAY ~ 22

"
Love doesn't command our obsession; love desires our heart.

DECEMBER: DAY ~ 23

"
The secret to love is to do unto others as you would have them do unto you.

DECEMBER: DAY ~ **24**

"
Love knows how to forgive the wrongs
and celebrate the rights.

DECEMBER: DAY ~ **25**

"
Let This Be The Season

Let this be the season you see His peace
  abound
In a world of much confusion, let His peace
  be found.

Let this be the season, His peace in you abide,
Knowing that you are eternally loved and
  right by His side.

Let this be the season you experience His
  perfect peace,
Safe in His arms, a peace that
  never cease.

Let this be the season that His peace
beckons you near,

To truly know the Prince of Peace each day
  of the year.

Let this be the season that His peace
  bombards your praise!
As you gaze upon the promised Son, His
  perfect gift, a magnificent love, O Ancient of
  Days!

_____

DECEMBER: DAY ~ **26**

"
   Mercy never forgets how to love.

_____

DECEMBER: DAY ~ **27**

"
   Love's passion was presented to us all,
bared all, consumed all; love became our all!

DECEMBER: DAY ~ **28**

" To gaze upon the truth of love allows our hearts to see God.

_____

DECEMBER: DAY ~ **29**

" Love's voice has no reason to shout; eternal peace is what true love is all about.

_____

DECEMBER: DAY ~ **30**

" No need to guess what love looks like because love looks like us. We were all created by love.

DECEMBER: DAY ~ 31

"
   True love is a costly sweet fragrance, like the ointment that vastly permeated from the Alabaster Box, our balm of Gilead, Jesus Christ.

The true precious aroma of the Father's heart is poured lavishly upon us all. These cups were made to run over. Love Pours!

WHEN LOVE POURS, LOVE SPEAKS

DAILY DEVOTION

- ABOUT THE AUTHOR -

Amanda Nabors, the "Quote Queen" is a multifaceted professional with a diverse range of talents and a strong spiritual calling. As an educator, she dedicates herself to nurturing and guiding young minds, imparting knowledge with a blend of patience and enthusiasm. Her passion for writing and poetry allows her to express her thoughts and emotions creatively, often exploring profound themes and personal experiences.

In addition to her literary pursuits, Amanda is also a skilled artist and songwriter, where she combines her artistic vision with melodious elements to craft unique and meaningful compositions. Her role as an ordained minister, intercessor, and motivational speaker highlights her ability to inspire and uplift others, drawing on her own life experiences and insights to encourage positive change and personal growth.

www.ingramcontent.com/pod-product-compliance
Lightning Source LLC
Chambersburg PA
CBHW051201120626
46547CB00012B/1156